D1064748

WEIRD AND WONDERFUL AIRCRAFT

Paul Eden

Please visit our web site at: www.garethstevens.com
For a free color catalog describing Gareth Stevens Publishing's list of high-quality books and multimedia programs, call 1-800-542-2595 (USA) or 1-800-387-3178 (Canada). Gareth Stevens Publishing's fax: (414) 332-3567.

Library of Congress Cataloging-in-Publication Data

Eden, Paul E.
Weird and wonderful aircraft / by Paul E. Eden.
p. cm. — (Aircraft of the world)
Includes bibliographical references and index.
ISBN-10: 0-8368-6906-0 — ISBN-13: 978-0-8368-9606-4 (lib. bdg.)
1. Research aircraft—Juvenile literature. I. Title. II. Series.
TL567.R47E34 2006
629.133'3—dc22 2006004071

This North American edition first published in 2007 by
Gareth Stevens Publishing
A Member of the WRC Media Family of Companies
330 West Olive Street, Suite 100
Milwaukee, WI 53212 USA

Produced by Amber Books Ltd., Bradley's Close,
74–77 White Lion Street, London N1 9PF, U.K.

Project Editor: Michael Spilling
Design: Brian Rust

Gareth Stevens editor: Carol Ryback
Gareth Stevens art direction: Tammy West
Gareth Stevens cover design: Scott M. Krall
Gareth Stevens production: Jessica Morris

Measurements appear in statute miles.

Printed in the United States of America

1 2 3 4 5 6 7 8 9 10 09 08 07 06

Cover and title page: Pilots liked the way the Frisbee-shaped V-173 handled, but the design never became popular.

Contents

Words that appear in the glossary are printed in **boldface** type the first time they occur in the text.

1929

Dornier Do X

- **Largest aircraft in the world for more than ten years**
- **Twelve engines**

The Do X had a massive wingspan of 157 feet (48 meters).

The Do X flew for the first time in 1929. It was a **flying boat** — it could only land and take off from water. At the time, it was the largest and most powerful aircraft in the world. The Do X used all twelve engines during flight, which was very unusual. The original engines were replaced with more powerful American-made Curtiss Conqueror engines for its historic Atlantic Ocean crossing.

ACTION DATA

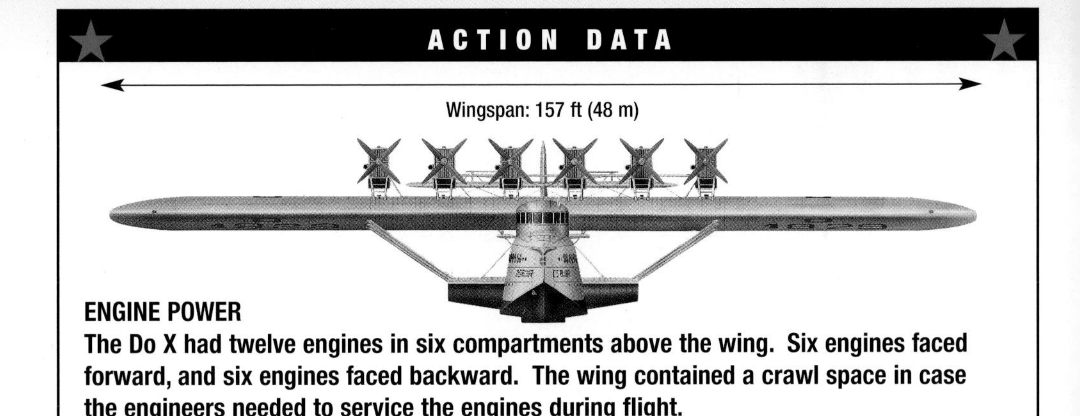

ENGINE POWER

The Do X had twelve engines in six compartments above the wing. Six engines faced forward, and six engines faced backward. The wing contained a crawl space in case the engineers needed to service the engines during flight.

Transatlantic Tour

As the Dornier Do X toured Europe, crowds appeared at every stop to view the unusual plane. The Dornier Do X continued on to Africa and then across the Atlantic Ocean to Natal, Brazil. From there it made its way north to New York City. Eighteen months after leaving Europe, the Dornier Do X finally arrived in Berlin, Germany. In 1934, the original Dornier Do X became a museum exhibit. Two more were built — for an Italian airline — but were not flown often. The first Dornier Do X was destroyed during a wartime air raid in 1945.

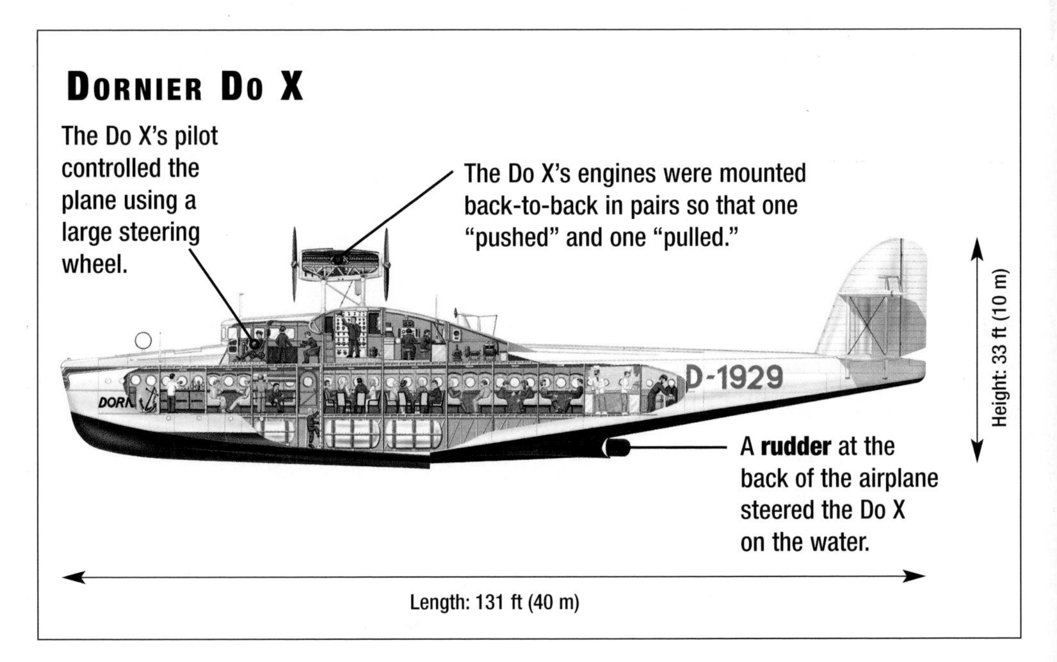

1938

Short Mayo Composite

- **Long-range floatplane and flying boat mothership**
- **Record-breaking flight**

***Maia* carried *Mercury* aloft on its back for launch in the air.**

By the 1930s, aircraft engineers had figured out how to launch small planes with overweight loads. Normally, a small plane with an overweight load could not take off safely. If a larger airplane launched a smaller one while in the air, however, the smaller one could carry a heavier than normal load.

Britain's Imperial Airways wanted to fly mail nonstop across the Atlantic Ocean, so it put a small floatplane on top of a large flying boat. The flying boat launched the floatplane, which then carried its load of mail across the ocean.

Mayo Composite

The Short Aircraft Company built the Mayo Composite. It was called a "composite" because it consisted of two aircraft teamed together. The Mayo was named after the man who came up with the design.

On August 21, 1938, the mothership — called *Maia* — launched the floatplane — named *Mercury* — on a trip to Canada from Ireland. *Mercury* carried so much mail and fuel that it could not have taken off on its own.

Later on that year, *Mercury* flew from Scotland to South Africa to set a world record for distance. No floatplane is ever likely to fly farther. World War II put an end to the Mayo Composite's transatlantic flights.

ACTION DATA

RECORD-BREAKING FLIGHT
***Mercury* flew from Scotland to South Africa — a journey of 6,000 miles (9,656 kilometers).**

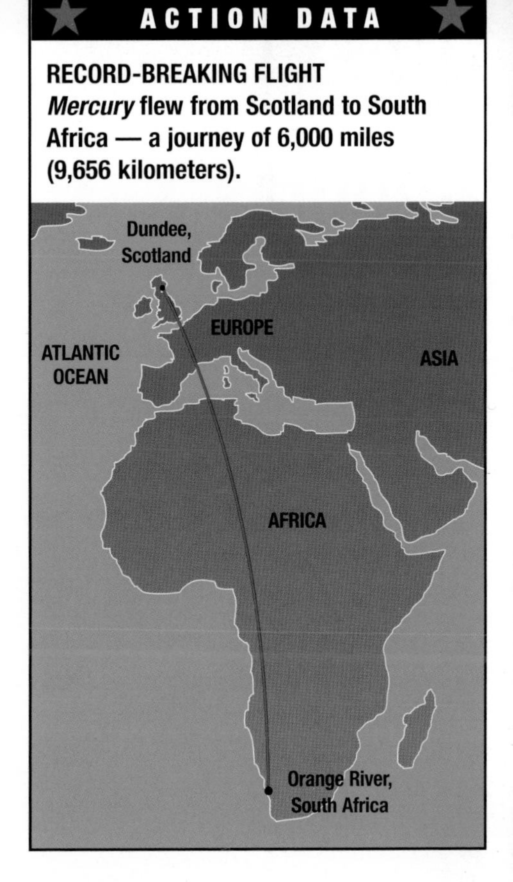

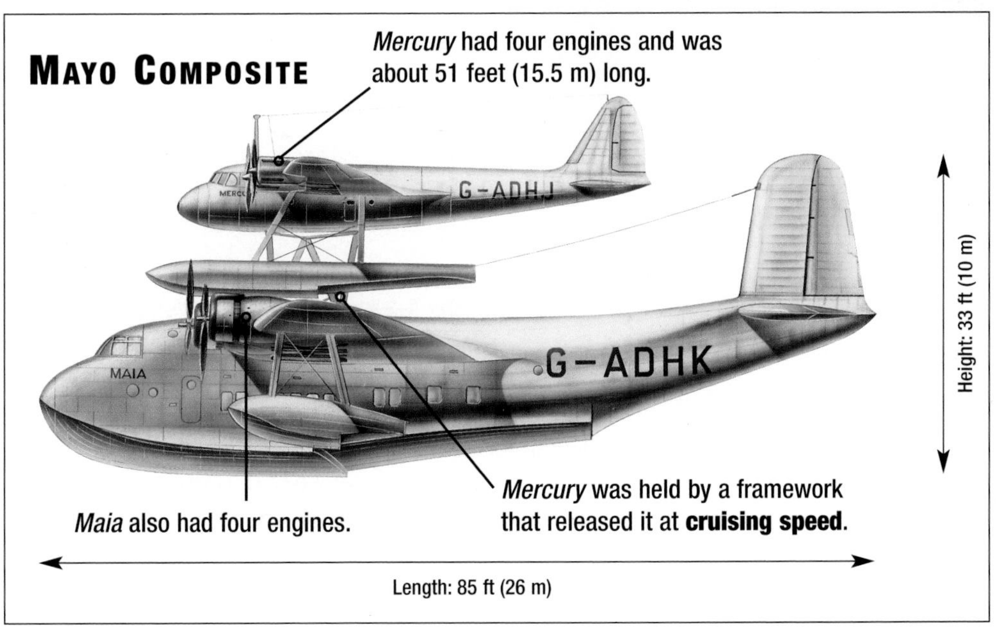

1943

Douglas X-3

- Designed for high-speed tests
- Made of aluminum, steel, and titanium

In December 1943, the U.S. government asked the Douglas Aircraft Company of Santa Monica, California, to build a test aircraft. This airplane, the X-3, had a long, thin shape and was equipped with many sensors that recorded temperatures and air pressures during high-speed flight. The recording instruments alone weighed about 1,200 pounds (544 kilograms). Douglas designed the X-3 to fly at **Mach 2** for thirty

The X-3 was designed to test the limits of high-speed flight.

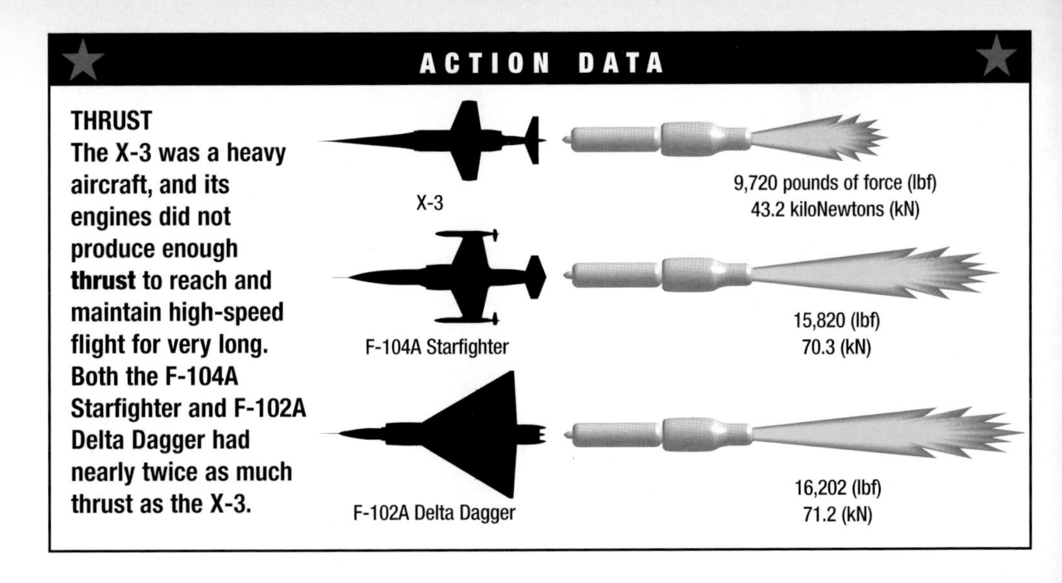

minutes. For the first time ever, parts of an airplane were built from **titanium**. Douglas also designed a new style of short, wide wings for the X-3.

Not Enough Power

The engines — two Westinghouse J46 engines — called for in the original design of the X-3 were not built in time, so Douglas installed two lower-powered J34 **turbojets** instead. As a result, the X-3 never had the power it was designed to have. The sleek X-3 could only reach speeds of Mach 1.1 in a dive. Still, the X-3 helped designers understand how to use titanium and helped engineers design other high-speed aircraft, such as the Lockheed F-104 Starfighter.

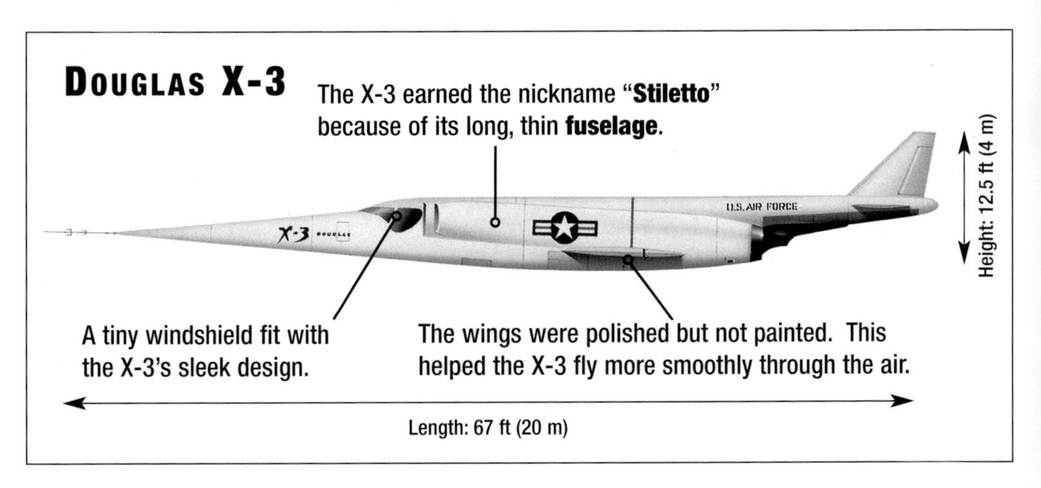

1947

Hughes H-4 Hercules

- **World's largest aircraft**
- **Transport flying boat**

As Howard Hughes flew his H-4 over Los Angeles Harbor, the plane never rose more than 82 feet (24 m) above the water.

In 1944, during World War II, the United States expected to transport thousands of soldiers and lots of heavy **cargo** to military bases scattered throughout the Pacific Ocean. Aviator Howard Hughes, along with shipbuilder Henry Kaiser, realized that a giant flying boat would be ideal for the job. Using some of Kaiser's money, Hughes designed and built the enormous H-4 Hercules. Many people called it the "Spruce Goose" because it was made from birch

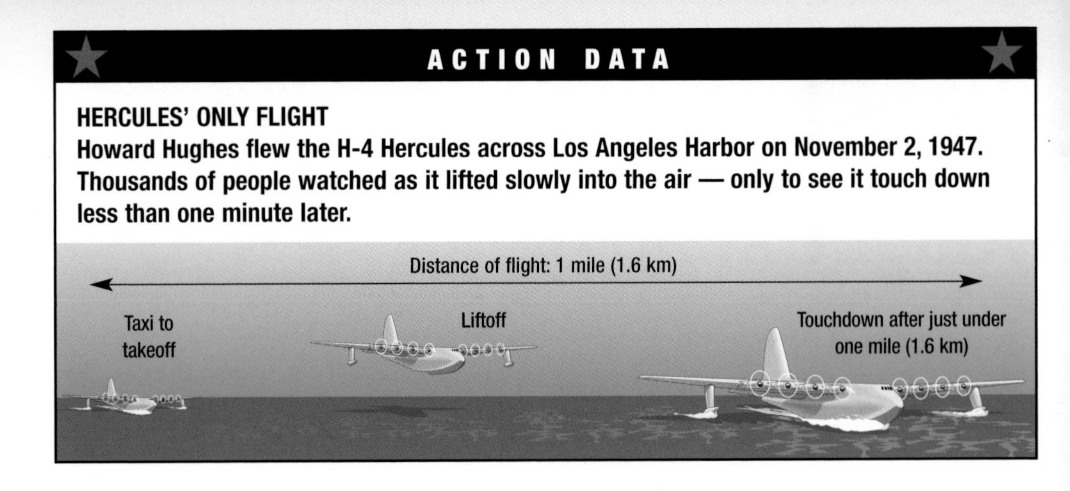

wood. Howard Hughes hated the "Spruce Goose" nickname.

Just One Flight

With eight engines and a wingspan of almost 320 feet (98 m), the H-4 was the largest airplane of its time by far. Hughes built it to carry 750 soldiers or 150,000 pounds (70,000 kg) of cargo.

On November 2, 1947, Hughes flew the Hercules for the first and only time. It flew for about 1 mile (1.6 km) across Los Angeles Harbor before landing.

For thirty years, the Hercules was the biggest flying machine ever built. The H-4 is now on display at the Evergreen Aviation Museum in McMinnville, Oregon.

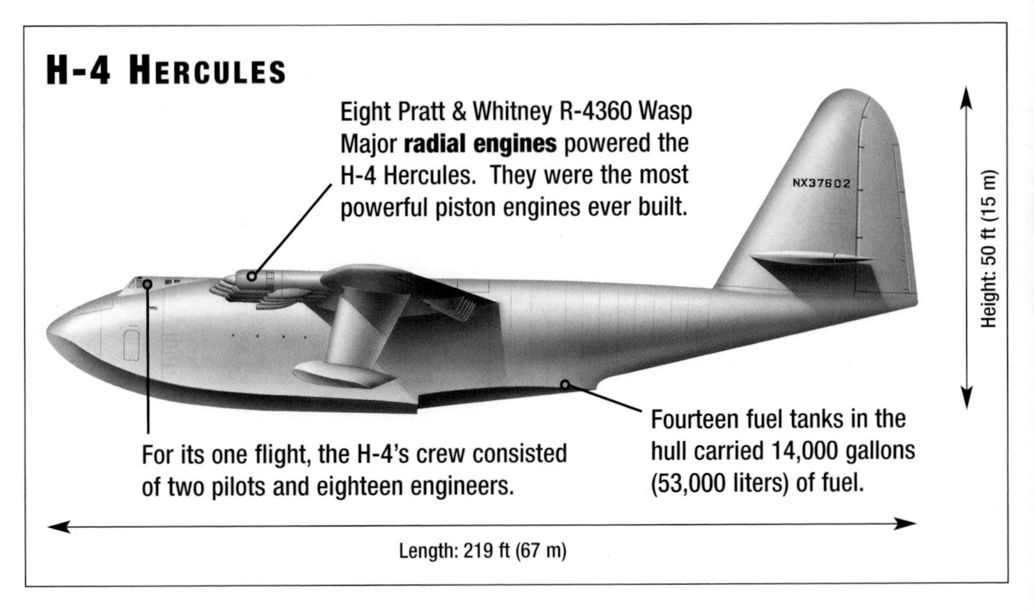

1947

Vought XF5U-1

- Experimental naval aircraft
- Round wing (called the "Flying Pancake")

Charles H. Zimmerman designed the V-173 with round wings for the Vought-Sikorsky Aircraft Company in Stratford, Connecticut. The V-173 looked like a Frisbee, but back then, people who helped build it referred to the aircraft as the "Zimmer Skimmer" or the "Flying Pancake." It first flew in 1943. The pilot entered the cockpit by climbing up a ladder and crawling through a trapdoor in the plane's belly. Pilots liked the way the V-173 handled, and even Charles

The XF5U-1 was designed as a Vertical Takeoff and Landing (VTOL) naval airplane.

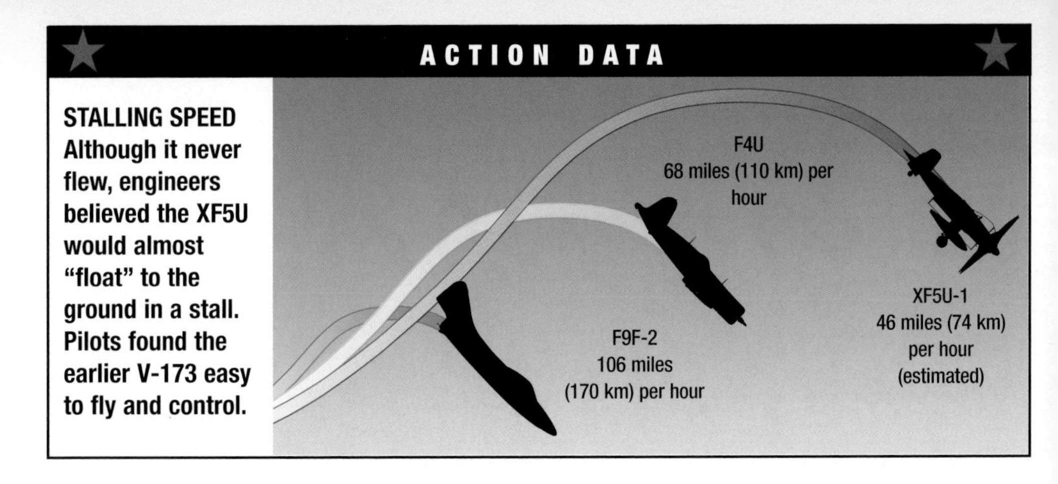

Lindbergh made several test flights. The V-173, which had an estimated speed range of from 48 miles (30 km) per hour to 500 miles (805 km) per hour, served as a model for the XF5U-1 naval aircraft.

"Flying Pancake"

The XF5U-1 "Flying Pancake" was made of lightweight balsa wood sandwiched between thin aluminum sheets. It was slightly bigger than the V-173 and had four enormous propellers instead of three. The XF5U-1 was designed to land and take off almost vertically on short runways, making it perfect for use on aircraft carriers. In March 1947, the XF5U-1 was cancelled. Jet aircraft were preferred over propeller-driven aircraft. The XF5U-1 never flew.

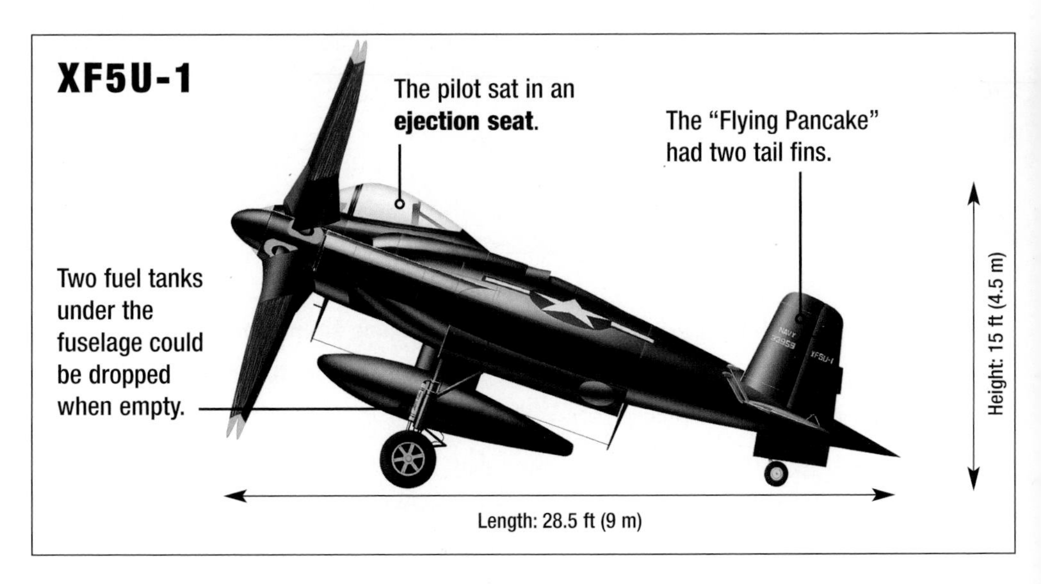

1953

Leduc 0.21 and 0.22

- **Experimental aircraft**
- **Ramjet engines**

Frenchman René Leduc experimented with **ramjets** (a special kind of jet engine). Ramjets can only start working after the plane is already flying. Wind gets "rammed" into the engine, which increases the pressure inside the engines and produces more thrust, or power.

A Languedoc airliner launched the Leduc 0.21 for test flying.

A Languedoc airplane carried the 0.21 into the air and released it for test flights.

An Engine for Flying Fast

Work then began on the O.22, which had a turbojet inside its ramjet. The turbojet powered the airplane to the correct speed for the ramjet to work. The O.22 could also take off by itself. Unfortunately, the O.22 was cancelled before its ramjet was ever used because it was considered too expensive.

The O.22 would have flown at Mach 2. A simpler Leduc O.10 with a normal jet engine flew at 500 miles (805 km) per hour using just half of its power.

ACTION DATA

THRUST
A ramjet increases the thrust of an airplane so that it reaches high speeds quickly. Most experimental aircraft used jet engines, which have less thrust.

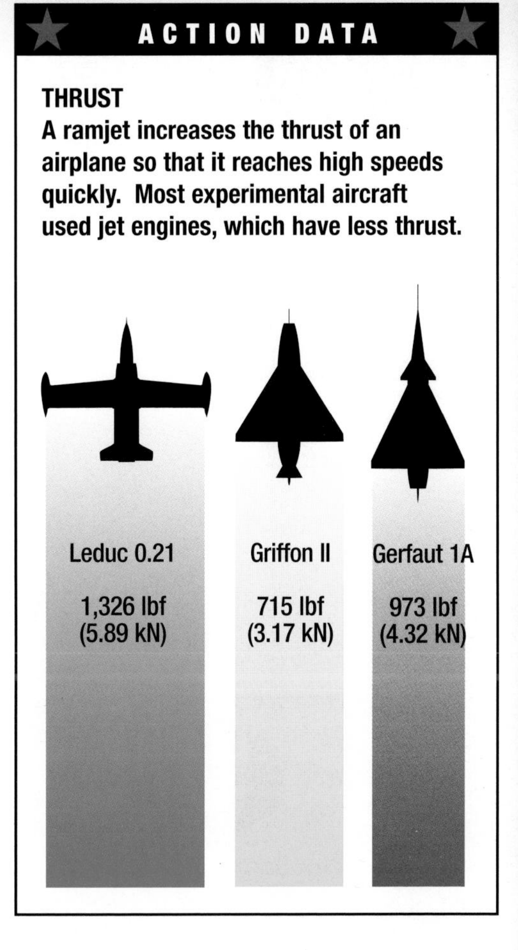

Leduc 0.21

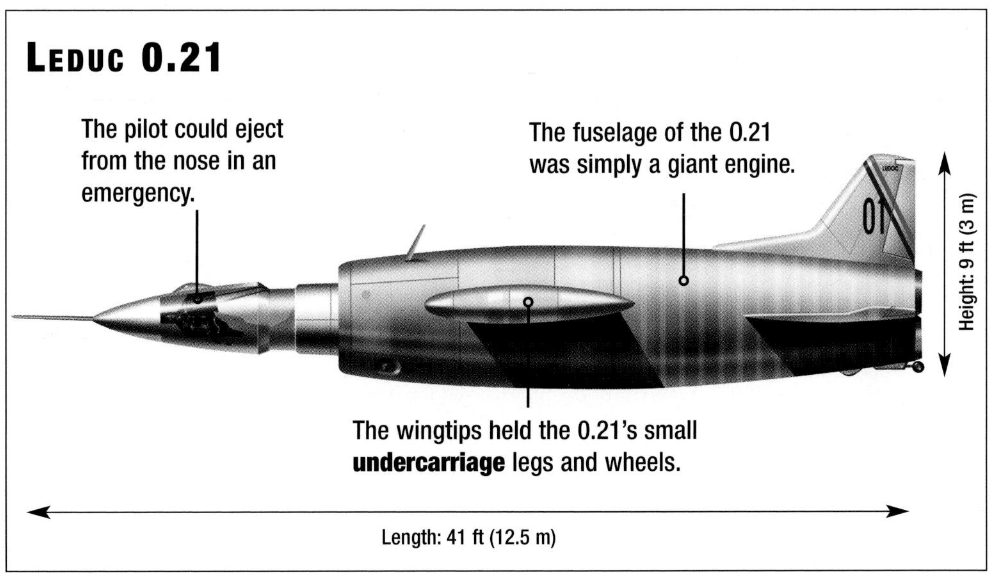

1953

Thrust Measuring Rig

- **Experimental VTOL (Vertical Takeoff and Landing) aircraft**
- **No wings or fuselage**

The Thrust Measuring Rig could hover for fifteen minutes.

Every year, jet engines became more powerful. By 1953, the best jets produced more thrust than they weighed, which meant that they could lift their own weight. Britain's Rolls-Royce Company realized that if two engines were installed in a simple framework with their thrust pointing downward, the aircraft would lift vertically. Rolls Royce engineers also realized that being able to lift off vertically could be very useful for military aircraft, especially those flying from aircraft carriers. Rolls-Royce called its aircraft the Thrust Measuring Rig.

ACTION DATA

TEST FLIGHT
Rolls Royce engineers and members of Britain's Royal Air Force (RAF) watch a test flight of the Thrust Measuring Rig, June 1954. Though the Rig never entered service, it showed the way for other vertical takeoff craft.

"Flying Bedstead"

Because of all the metal tubes used in its design, the Thrust Measuring Rig looked like an old iron bed. Its nickname was the "Flying Bedstead." The thrust from its two engines lifted it straight up.

Rolls-Royce proved that a VTOL aircraft did not have to be a helicopter. The "Flying Bedstead" helped Rolls-Royce design the Harrier Jump Jet. Two "Flying Bedsteads" were built between 1953 to 1957. Both crashed.

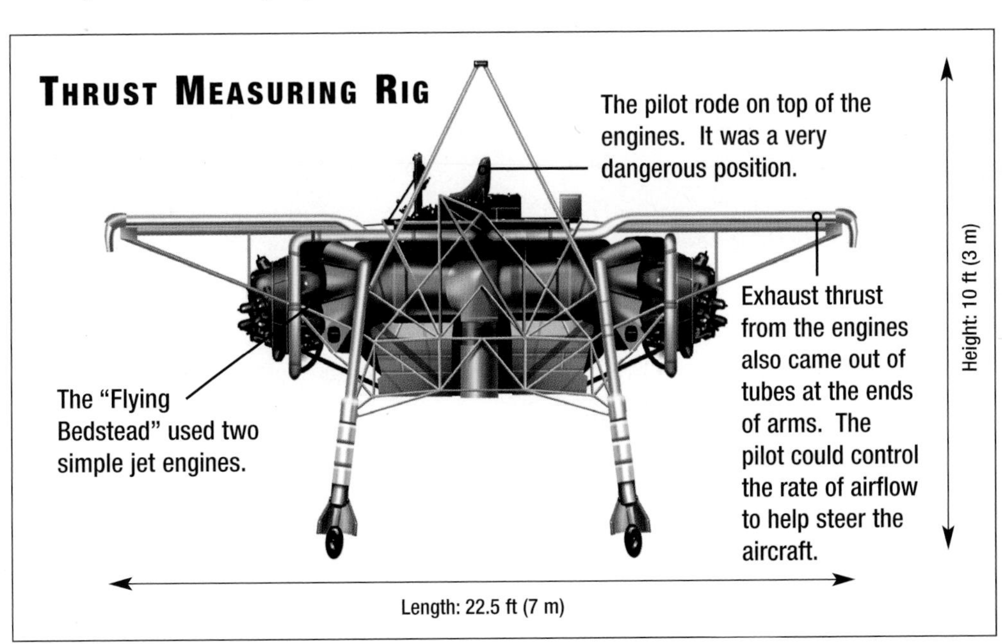

1957

Fairey Rotodyne

- **Compound helicopter**
- **Designed as an airliner**

The Rotodyne looked like a cross between a helicopter and an airplane.

In 1951, British European Airways wanted an airliner that could take off and land vertically. It had to be able to fly directly into the middle of a city, carry forty passengers, and be faster than a helicopter. Fairey, a British aircraft maker, had been working on a compound helicopter — a helicopter with **turboprop** engines for forward flight and a large **main rotor** for vertical takeoff and landing. In 1957,

Fairey flew its compound helicopter, called the Rotodyne, for the first time.

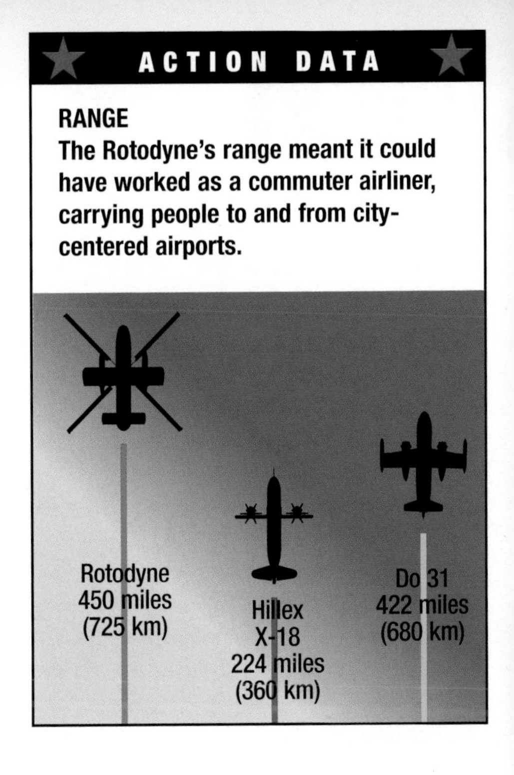

Complicated and Too Heavy

The Rotodyne had two turboprop engines to turn its propellers. The engines also produced **compressed air** that was blown out of jets at the tips of the helicopter's rotor blades to give the helicopter extra lift power. This complicated design made the Rotodyne faster than any other helicopter of its time.

The Rotodyne was very heavy and required powerful engines for takeoff. Some airlines placed orders for the Rotodyne, but then cancelled them when it became clear that this model was extremely heavy and very expensive to build and operate. Production of the Rotodyne was stopped in 1962.

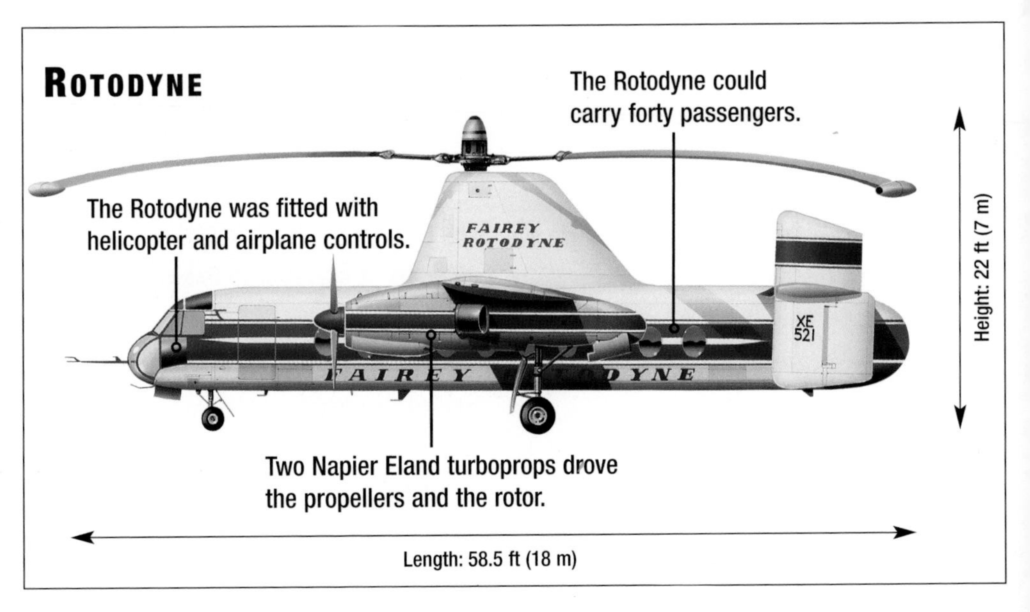

1958

Northrop X-4

- **Experimental aircraft with no stabilizers**
- **Used in NACA tests**

By 1946, NACA — the National Advisory Committee for Aeronautics, which later became the National Aeronautics and Space Administration (NASA) — had realized that, at **transonic** speeds, shockwaves from an airplane's wing interfered with its **stabilizers**. To try to solve this problem, NACA asked Northrop Aircraft to develop and test a new aircraft. Northrop built two X-4 "tail-less" airplanes with no stabilizers that could fly at transonic speeds.

The X-4 was a very successful research airplane. It first flew in December 1958.

Useful Research

Northrop used its knowledge of the German Messerschmitt Me 163 and the British DH.108 Swallow to design the X-4. Pilots and others gave the tiny X-4s the nickname "Bantam" (a bantam is a small breed of chicken). Many pilots flew the X-4s, including Chuck Yeager. Two turbojets powered the Bantams, which flew at about Mach 0.88 (630 mph/1,013 kph).

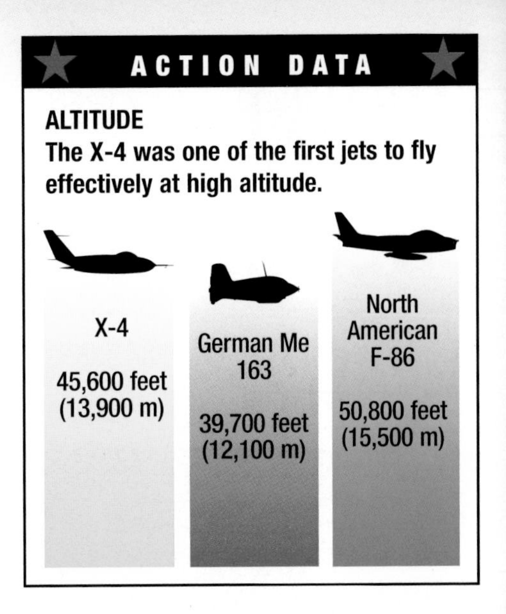

Both X-4 aircraft flew many times. The information Northrop collected proved that tail-less airplanes were not good for flying at transonic speeds. The pilots had no problem with shockwaves, but found that the aircraft were hard to control above speeds of Mach 0.88. Today, one of the X-4s is in the U.S. Air Force Museum in Wright-Patterson, Ohio. The other is at the U.S. Air Force Academy in Colorado Springs, Colorado.

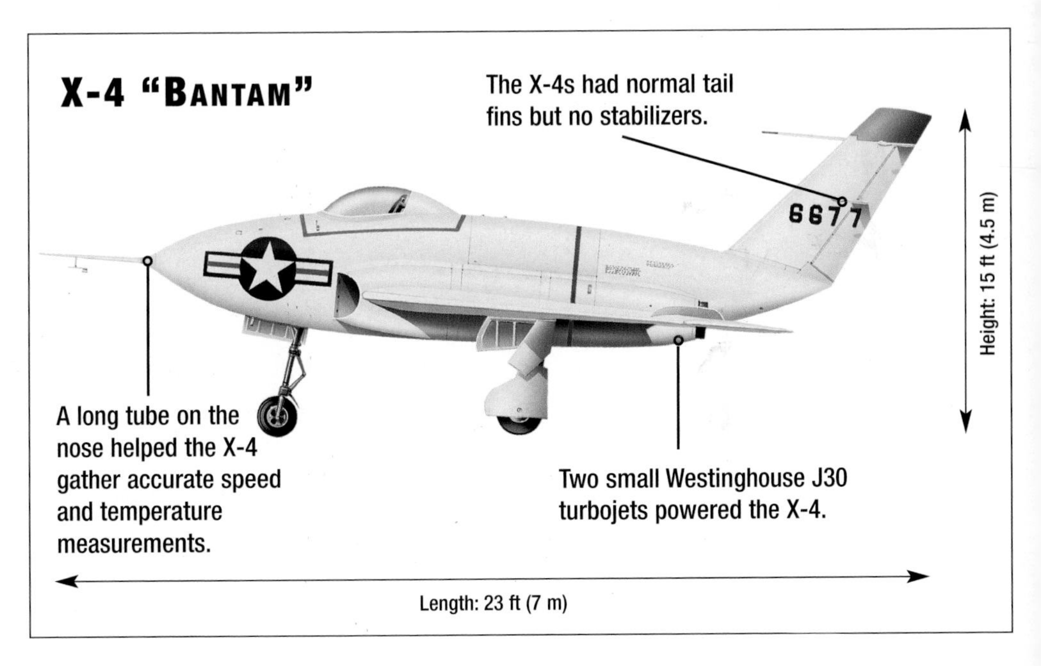

1959

SNECMA Coléoptère

- **Experimental VTOL (Vertical Takeoff and Landing) aircraft**
- **Ring-shaped wing**

The Coléoptère lifted off vertically. Wheels on its tail fins helped it roll on the ground.

In the 1950s, SNECMA, a major French aircraft engine manufacturer, was developing aircraft that used turbojet engines to take off and land vertically. At first, these aircraft were remote-controlled. When these were successful, a piloted aircraft was developed. Called the Coléoptère, it first flew in May 1959. The Coléoptère had a

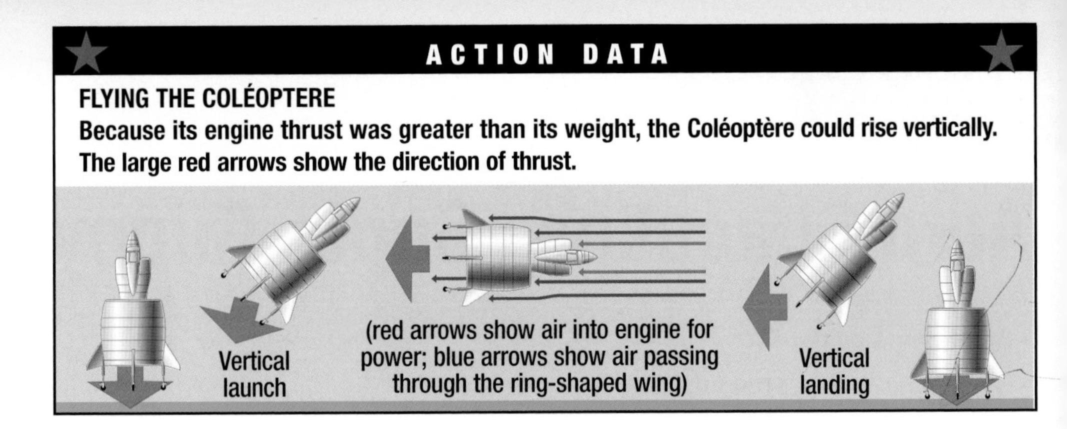

normal fuselage with a jet engine inside, but the wing was shaped like a ring. The ring-shaped wing went all the way around the fuselage.

Sitting On Its Tail

On the ground, the Coléoptère sat on multi-directional wheels on its "tail." It took off vertically, nose first, and landed nose last, with the pilot looking at the ground over his shoulder. The Coléoptère had many vertical test flights.

The pilot could also direct the engine thrust so that the airplane flew straight and level like a normal airplane. On July 25, 1959, the only time a pilot ever tried to make it fly straight, **hover**, and then land, the Coléoptère crashed.

Although it was one of the strangest aircraft ever made, the weaknesses of the Coléoptère finally proved that **VTOL** research was a dead end.

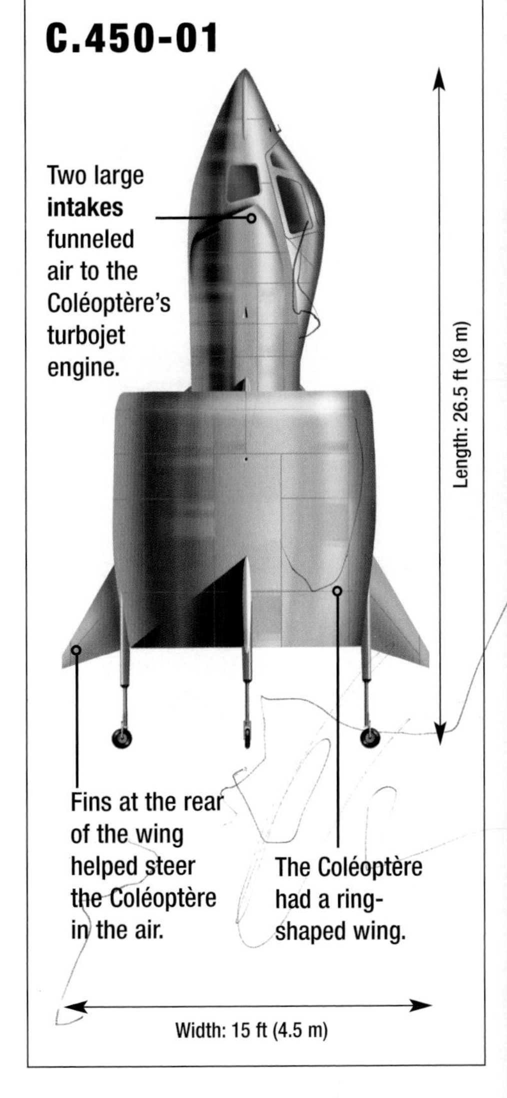

1962

Aero Spacelines Super Guppy

- **Giant cargo hold**
- **Opening nose for cargo loading**

Airbus relied on the Guppy 201 to carry airliner parts around Europe.

In 1960, aircraft designer Jack Conroy presented his idea for a huge cargo aircraft to NASA. He wanted to add a giant cargo **hold** to an old Boeing Stratocruiser airliner. Conroy thought such an aircraft would be able to carry NASA's rockets from Huntington Beach, California — where they were built and tested — to their launch site at Cape Canaveral, Florida.

A Guppy Family

Conroy's giant **freighter** first flew in 1962. It had a fat upper fuselage and was called the "**Guppy**" after a

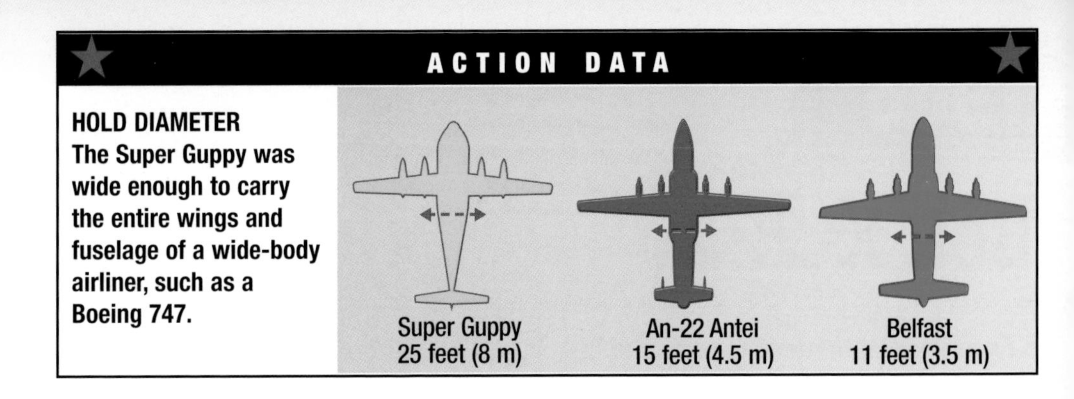

tiny fish. Though it moved many rocket parts around the United States, the Guppy was not big enough to carry the third stage of the enormous Saturn V rocket.

A Super Guppy, with a bigger hold and four turboprop engines, transported the space shuttle around the United States.

Meanwhile, Airbus Industrie, an association of European aircraft companies based in France, needed a large airplane. Airbus chose to use a new version of the Super Guppy — the Guppy 201. Four Guppy 201s served from 1973 to 1997.

In the United States, the last Guppy 201 is still in service with NASA. In Europe, the SATIC Beluga jet transport replaced the Guppy in the late 1990s.

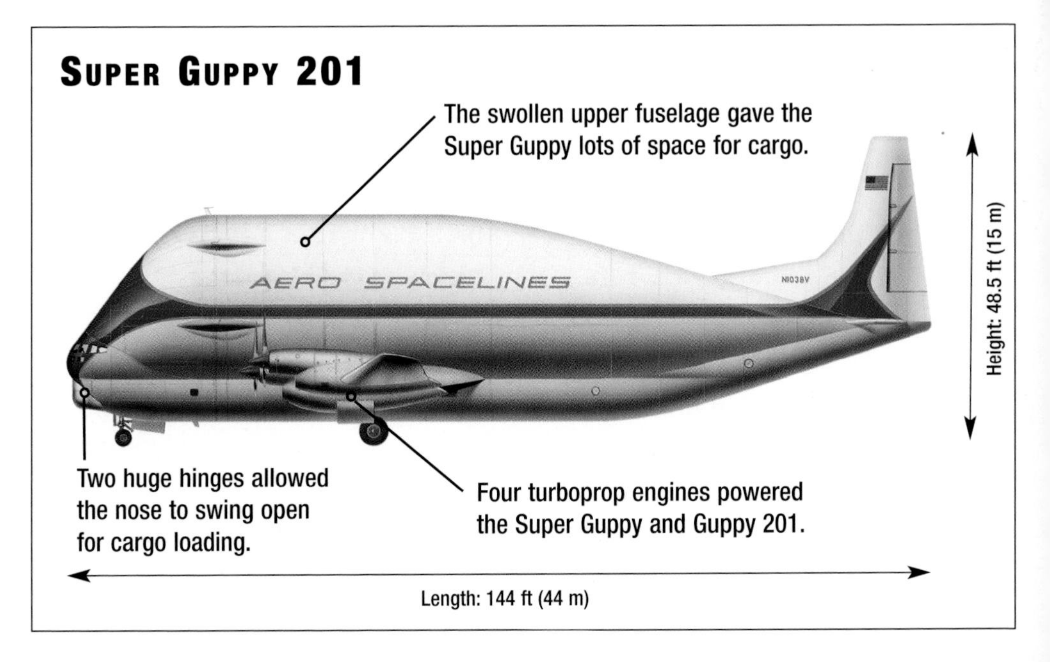

1966

Bell X-22A

- **Experimental Vertical Takeoff and Landing (VTOL) aircraft**
- **Powered by ducted propellers**

The X-22A could take off vertically — straight up like a helicopter.

Bell Aircraft Corporation wanted to test an aircraft that could land and take off vertically, with the shortest **ground roll** possible. Bell also wanted to test ducted propellers.

A ducted propeller is a normal propeller that turns inside a round case, or duct. The duct helps to lift the plane, which keeps the aircraft flying, and prevents people on the ground from being injured by the propellers.

Two Aircraft Built

Two X-22As were built. The first flew on March 17, 1966, but was soon destroyed in a crash. On July 30, 1968, the second aircraft achieved a hover at 8,018 feet (2,444 m) — a world record for any type of VTOL aircraft. This aircraft flew until 1984.

The position of the X-22A's four ducted propellers could be changed in flight — they could point up and down, or they could point from front to back. With the ducts pointing downward, the airplane could hover. When they were turned to face backward, the airplane flew forward.

The X-22A proved that a VTOL aircraft with ducted propellers could work. The second X-22A is on display at the Niagara Aerospace Museum in Niagara Falls, New York.

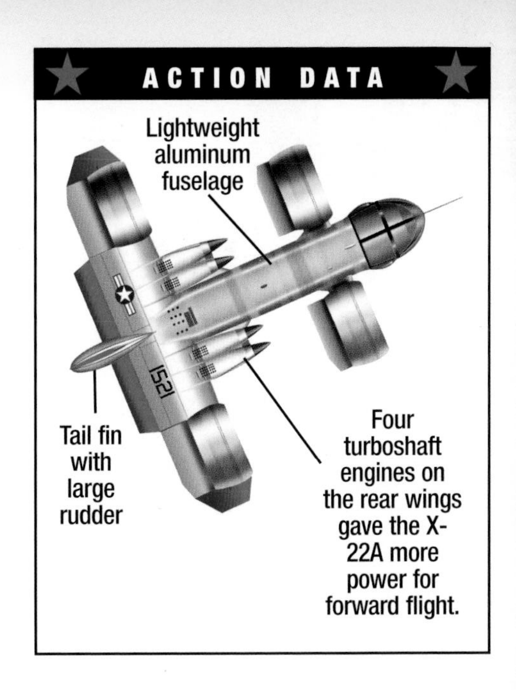

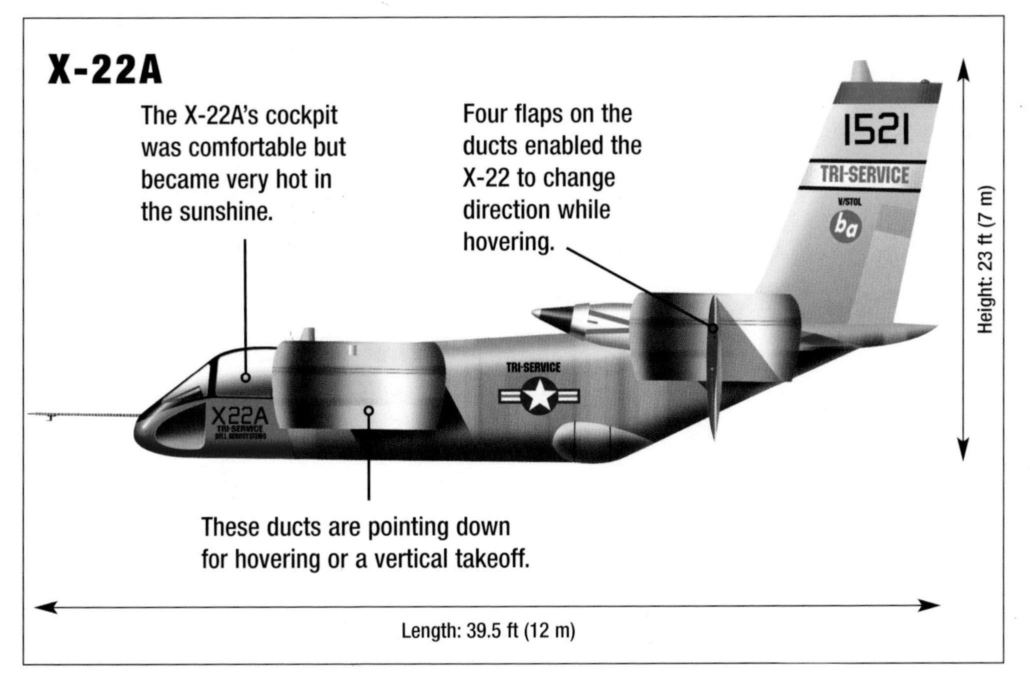

1979

Ames-Dryden AD-1

- **Pivot-wing research aircraft**
- **Used in NASA experiments**

A view from below shows the wing in "scissors" position for high-speed flight.

For takeoff and landing, the best wing is a straight one. For high-speed flight, the best wing is at an angle. Aircraft such as the Grumman F-14 Tomcat use **swing wings**, which are positioned straight for takeoff and "swept" for fast flying. These wings are heavy and expensive to make. NASA wanted to try a cheaper version, so it designed the AD-1, with a **pivoting** wing. The wing was held straight for takeoff and pivoted — so that one wing was swept forward and the other wing was swept back — for high-speed flight. It was called a "scissors" wing design.

The AD-1 was just 38 feet (12 m) long and very lightweight. NASA used the AD-1 from 1979 to 1982.

Successful Tests

NASA's Ames Research Center built the AD-1. It was a small airplane with two jet engines. In tests, the AD-1 was very successful. NASA wanted to put the same type of wing on its F-8 Crusader fighter to test the wing at **supersonic** speeds. Unfortunately, that design proved too expensive. Today, NASA is again looking at pivot-wing designs as it develops aircraft for the future.

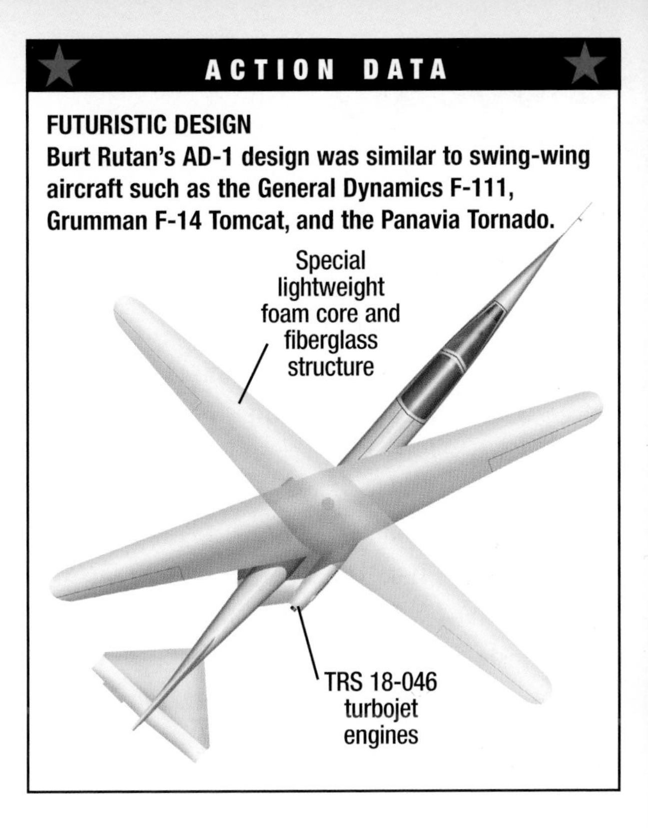

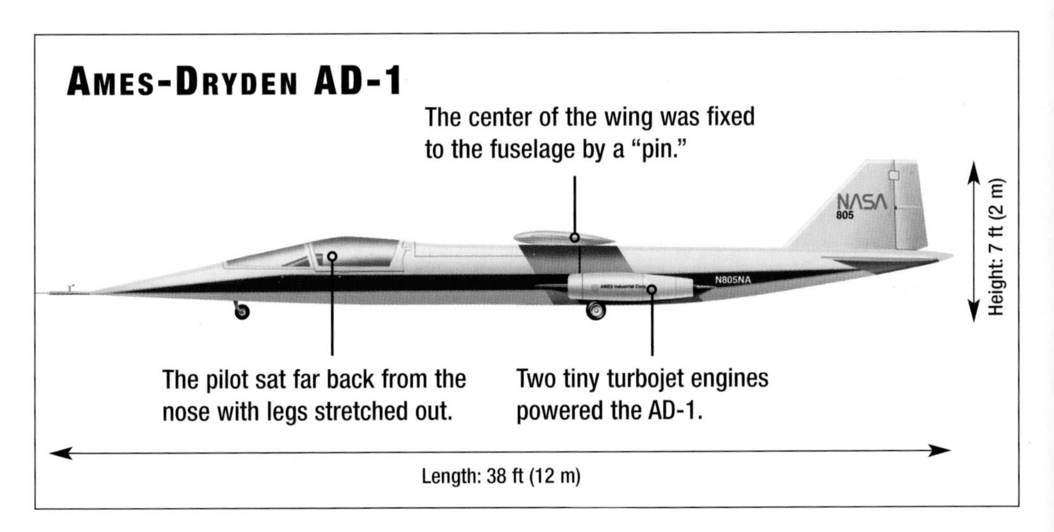

Glossary

cargo — goods and equipment carried by an aircraft or other vehicle
compressed air — air that is "squeezed" so that it can be blown out of a jet
cruising speed — the speed an aircraft can fly at for any length of time
drag — a force that slows down an aircraft or other vehicle
ejection seat — a safety seat that helps a pilot exit in an emergency
floatplane — an aircraft with floats for landing and taking off from water
flying boat — an aircraft with a boat-shaped fuselage for landing and taking off from water
freighters — aircraft that carry cargo
fuselage — the main body of an airplane
ground roll — the distance an aircraft travels along the ground before taking off
guppy — a fish with a swollen belly
hold — where cargo is carried in an aircraft
hover — to remain in one place in while airborne
intakes — holes in the outside of an aircraft that bring air into the engine
Mach 2 — twice the speed of sound (Mach 1 is the speed of sound — 760 miles/1,223 km per hour)
main rotor — the large spinning blades that make a helicopter fly
pivoting — turning around a fixed point
radial engines — engines with cylinders arranged in spokes, like a bike wheel
ramjets — jet engines that work by ingiting fuel mixed with compressed air
rudder — a plate of metal or wood mounted on the back of an aircraft that moves the aircraft tail from side to side
stabilizers — the horizontal (flat) surfaces at an aircraft's tail that keep it steady
stiletto — a long, thin heel on a woman's shoe
supersonic — faster than the speed of sound
swing wings — swept back wings that can change position in flight
thrust — the force from a jet engine that makes an airplane move
titanium — a strong, light metal that does not rust easily
transonic — speeds at or near the speed of sound
turbojets — simple jet engines
turboprop — a jet engine that turns a propeller
undercarriage — the legs, wheels, skis, or skids that an airplane uses for landing
VTOL — Vertical Takeoff and Landing — the ability to take off and land in an upright position without a runway

For More Information

Books

Amazing Agricultural Aircraft. Timothy R. Gaffney. (Enslow)

Seaplanes: And Naval Aviation. The Story of Flight (series).
Ole Steen Hansen (Crabtree)

The Story of Flight: Early Flying Machines, Balloons, Blimps, Gliders, Warplanes, and Jets. Voyages of Discovery (series).
Dan Hagedorn and Sheila Keenan (editors) (Scholastic)

Weird & Wonderful Aircraft. The Story of Flight (series).
Ole Steen Hansen (Crabtree)

Web sites

Dryden Flight Research Center
Shows images of the AD-1 in flight.
www.nasa.gov/centers/dryden/history/pastprojects/AD1/index.html

Unreal Aircraft — SNECMA Coléoptère
Photographs and information on the workings and history of the SNECMA Coléoptère.
www.unrealaircraft.com/gravity/snecmaC450-01.php

Evergreen Aviation Museum
A guide to a museum dedicated to classic American aircraft.
www.sprucegoose.org

Weird and wonderful aircraft at the National Museum of the United States Air Force
A tour of some of the strangest military and civil aircraft made in the U.S.
www.richard-seaman.com/Aircraft/Museums/Dayton/Oddities

Publisher's note to educators and parents: Our editors have carefully reviewed these Web sites to ensure that they are suitable for children. Many Web sites change frequently, however, and we cannot guarantee that a site's future contents will continue to meet our high standards of quality and educational value. Be advised that children should be closely supervised whenever they access the Internet.

Index